The Sports Book of
Windsurfing

John Leaf

Frederick Warne

Published by
Frederick Warne (Publishers) Ltd
40 Bedford Square
London WC1B 3HE

First published 1981
Reprinted 1982

ISBN 0 7232 3016 1

Printed and bound in Great Britain by
Galava Printing Company Ltd, Nelson, Lancs

CONTENTS

INTRODUCTION

ABOUT THIS SERIES

Venture Guides are written for the guidance and instruction of all those who enjoy active leisure pursuits, and they fall into two broad areas.

The first group covers such basic but essential outdoor skills as Knot-tying, Map reading and Compass work, Camping and Cooking skills, Weather Lore, First Aid, and Survival and Rescue techniques. These are the skills which all outdoor people should possess. A full list of such titles will be found in the front of this book.

The second group covers what we describe as Venture Sports. These are activities which do not require mechanical assistance and are not team games. This group therefore includes such activities as Rock Climbing, Hill Walking, Backpacking, Snorkelling, Sailing, Downhill and Cross Country Skiing, and Canoeing, and again, a list is at the front of the book.

To this second group we now add this book, an introductory guide to the exciting and fast-growing sport of Boardsailing.

ABOUT THIS BOOK

Boardsailing, or Windsurfing as it is often (incorrectly) called, is the world's fastest growing water sport. Since the middle Sixties sail-boards have appeared in increasing numbers all over the waters, and the sport has grown from an eccentric hobby to an Olympic event.

This book lays out the basics of boardsailing in a clear, readable manner, explaining the theory, giving advice on technique, and in a series of illustrations, showing how the beginner can start to sail and progress swiftly and safely to a mastery of the sport.

Chapter 1

THE HISTORY AND DEVELOPMENT OF BOARDSAILING

The first few attempts at boardsailing (or windsurfing) can be frustrating, putting off many a beginner. This book is intended to explain away some of the myths attached to the sport and help the beginner over the first ten hours or so, which are, perhaps, the most important period. It is not intended as a substitute for instruction at a recognised Boardsailing School (undoubtedly the best way of learning the sport), but rather as a guide, a helping hand, a book to consult and study before or after completing a course with a competent instructor, or when attempting to teach yourself.

There are many varying opinions on 'how to do it standing up' and this is an attempt to take into account the recognised teaching method practised and perfected over many years in many parts of the world, plus a personal viewpoint based on years of experience in teaching absolute beginners of all age groups, all shapes and sizes and all walks of life, and starting them off on the right 'wave' to discover the wonderful new world of Boardsailing.

Boardsailing, or windsurfing as it is now often called, is to Sailing what Hang-gliding is to flying aeroplanes. It is something unique. It has been described, I think very aptly, as 'the ultimate free ride'.

HISTORY

The 'Windsurfer', the first sailboard, originated in North America in 1967. The idea originated from two Californians, Hoyle Schweitzer and Jim Drake, who decided to combine the joys of sailing with the thrill of surfing. Naturally, the surfer's paradise, Hawaii, was the scene of most of the development of the Windsurfer, and in fact still is. The designer, Hoyle Schweitzer, probably never dreamed that this new and exciting sport would have the universal acceptance and success which it has achieved today as the fastest developing water sport.

Boardsailing, windsurfing or sailboarding — whatever you like to call it — is, above all, fun. It enables anyone who is reasonably fit (and able to swim), from the age of seven to seventy, to enjoy the freedom of the sea and the surf, using only the wind for propulsion. In fact, one of the beauties of this form of sailing is that virtually any stretch of water is sufficient, providing there is wind and room to manoeuvre.

The board needs no mooring, requires no trailer, can be easily lifted on or off a car roof-rack, and can be rigged in five minutes and carried easily to and from the water by one person. Boardsailing is, in this respect, a truly individual sport.

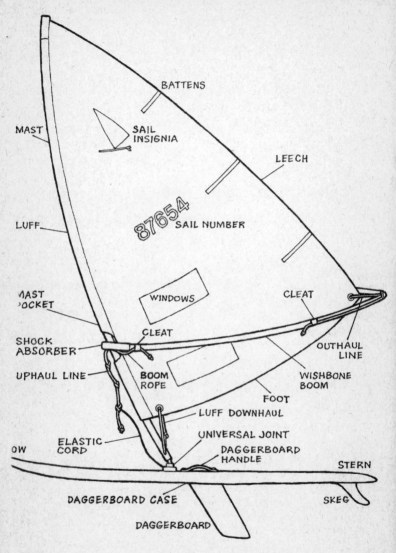

BATTENS

MAST

SAIL INSIGNIA

LEECH

LUFF

87654 SAIL NUMBER

MAST POCKET

CLEAT

SHOCK ABSORBER

CLEAT

WINDOWS

OUTHAUL LINE

UPHAUL LINE

BOOM ROPE

WISHBONE BOOM

FOOT

LUFF DOWNHAUL

ELASTIC CORD

UNIVERSAL JOINT

OW

DAGGERBOARD HANDLE

STERN

DAGGERBOARD CASE

SKEG

DAGGERBOARD

Fig. 1

6

The board can be sailed either in light winds, yet still move fairly quickly, or in strong winds (by an experienced sailor) when it can attain speeds of twenty knots or more — faster than any other single hulled sailing craft!

EQUIPMENT

The standard sailboard consists of:

The Board (or Hull), which is about twelve feet in length (different brands will vary slightly) and about two and a half feet wide and five inches thick. It is made from polyethylene, glass-fibre, A.B.S. plastic, or sometimes plywood. Usually the outer shell is filled with foam to give it buoyancy and the bare board weighs around 22 kilos (45 pounds). It has one, two or even three 'wells' into which the 'mast-foot' slots. Behind this there is a slot for the daggerboard, known as the daggerboard case. Underneath, at the back of the board, there is a small fin or 'skeg' which is normally detachable.

The Mast is made from either glass-fibre or aluminium, and is hollow and flexible. It is usually about fourteen feet long, and has a rounded 'plug' at the top and a mast-foot assembly with a universal joint at the bottom (see Fig. 2).

The Boom (or Wishbone) is attached to the mast at shoulder height and curves around both sides of the sail. It is made from either

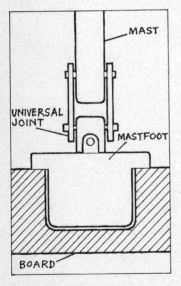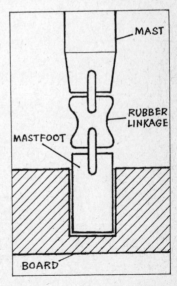

Fig. 2

aluminium or wood and can be round, oval, square, or even hex-
agonal in section, offering a wide variety of hand-grips. It should have
a shock-absorber at the front to avoid damaging the board when the
'rig' (mast, boom and sail together) falls on it, and should have a
strong but soft-textured rope attached to the front end. This is known
as the 'uphaul line', and is used for pulling the sail up out of the water.
It also has another thinner line known as the 'outhaul', attached to
the other end, and this is used for tightening or loosening the sail.
(See Fig. 3.) *The Sail* is made from terylene sailcloth and is slotted
over the mast with a sleeve on the leading edge or luff. The normal
sail is about 5.6 sq. metres in area but there are differing sizes and
shapes for varying wind-strengths, as well as small sails for beginners
or for children.

Most sails are distinguished by their bright bands of colour, as well
as by an emblem denoting the class or make of board plus a sail-
number. They also have a transparent plastic window through which
the sailor can see what is happening on the other side of the sail. The
larger sails contain three battens, made from either wood or plastic,
which stiffen the trailing edge (leech) and keep the sail in shape. On
smaller sails these are not necessary as the leech is cut differently.

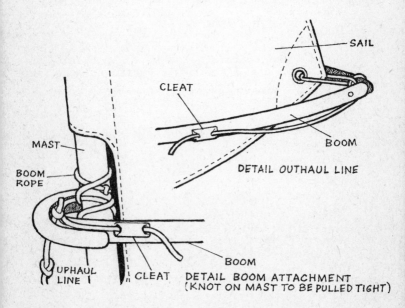

Fig. 3

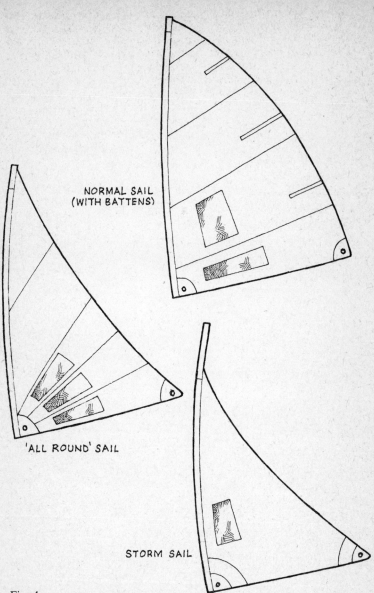

NORMAL SAIL
(WITH BATTENS)

'ALL ROUND' SAIL

STORM SAIL

Fig. 4

9

Sails can be classified as follows (see Fig. 4):

Light-weather Sail: This is a sail for use by experts in light winds and in 'open' regattas. It can be as large as 8 sq.m.

Standard Size Sail: For normal use, 5.2 to 5.8 sq.m. (54–58 sq.ft.).

All-round Sail: About 4.5 to 5 sq.m. It has no battens and a curved leech and is used in stronger winds, or by beginners.

Storm Sail: Very small and double-stitched in order to withstand gale-force winds. About 4 sq.m.

The Daggerboard or Centreboard is made from either plastic or wood and is about two feet long. It slots through the daggerboard case and has a strap, made from rope, plastic or canvas, which is used for pulling it up or out. The daggerboard stops the sailboard from drifting sideways. There are various shapes and types for use in different conditions, such as high wind, surf, shallow water etc. The wooden type should be kept smooth by sanding down and giving it a coat of varnish or paint from time to time. (See Fig. 5.)

The sailboard should be kept as free from unnecessary gadgets as possible. The great thing about boardsailing is simplicity, and the equipment listed above is all that the sailboard needs.

SAFETY

Provided that some basic rules are adhered to, boardsailing can be regarded as a safe sport. However, it is important to remember that when you are sailing on the sea, the sea should always be respected. It is forever changing, and therefore it is imperative that the sailor is aware of the prevailing weather conditions and can recognise his or her own limitations. Going out in a strong wind **alone** is dangerous, even if you know how to sail well. Venturing out without supervision, without someone keeping an eye on you from the shore, is also not to be recommended. Sailing with an *off-shore* wind, one blowing off the land, is usually exciting as the water is flat, but it can also be dangerous when you get tired or if something breaks, for you will drift away from the shore and may not be able to get back.

Never sail near a crowded beach, near swimmers or in shipping lanes, and never in areas where there are strong tides or currents, unless you are well aware of how they operate, or better still, have a reliable motor-boat for company. Having said this (which would equally apply to sailing dinghies), there are a few more rules which should be adhered to:

1. If you intend to sail in rough sea or open water always make sure that the mast is attached to the board with a line so that when (not if) you fall in and the mast-foot comes out of the slot in the board, it will not part company and drift away.

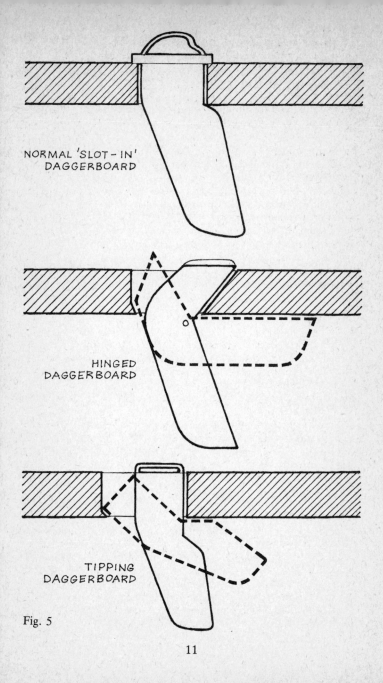

NORMAL 'SLOT-IN'
DAGGERBOARD

HINGED
DAGGERBOARD

TIPPING
DAGGERBOARD

Fig. 5

11

2. Always carry some spare line with you (tied around the boom for instance), with which you can make the odd repair while at sea.

3. Make sure you know how to tie the essential knots (bowline, rolling-hitch, reef-knot etc.) and, perhaps more important, how to **untie** them under severe conditions.

4. You should know how to wrap up the sail correctly and lay the rig on the board, so that if you have to paddle the board home either lying or kneeling on the board, using hands or daggerboard as paddles, the sail doesn't become an encumbrance.

5. The internationally recognised signal for boardsailors requiring help is to sit on the board and cross the arms above the head (see Fig. 6). The board will not move far with the sail in the water because the sail acts as a sea-anchor, but once the sail is wrapped tightly around the mast and the rig then laid on top of the board, the craft becomes much more manageable and can be paddled fairly quickly.

6. Never attempt to paddle the board while the sail is in the water. It is very hard work and you will not make much progress.

As a matter of courtesy, try not to get mixed up with dinghy fleets at regattas; this is a sure way to make yourself unpopular. They will discover boardsailing for themselves sooner or later!

FALLING IN

When you feel that you are about to fall, don't hang on until the very last moment. Try to jump or fall in on the opposite side to the sail. If you do fall on the wrong side, and the sail is lying in the water to windward, climb on to the board, take hold of the uphaul line and swivel the board around, your feet next to the mast, by leaning the mast towards either the front or the back of the board until you have it facing in the direction you want it to go, with the sail to leeward (away from the wind). Take your time, work out the wind direction and check your position (feet, back, shoulders, arms and hands) and don't be bothered by people laughing at you when you fall in — it's unlikely that they could do any better!

It is important to remember that the board will not sink, so stay with it. Do not try swimming ashore **without** the board if you find yourself in trouble — it is probably further than you think!

Finally, learn to swim really well; and even a competent swimmer would be well advised to wear a lifejacket.

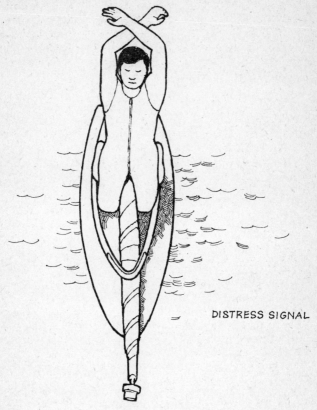

DISTRESS SIGNAL

Fig. 6

Chapter 2

WHICH BOARD?

Choosing the right board has become more difficult as the sport has gained in popularity. Years ago there were very few boards on the market, whereas now there are hundreds, and new brands appear almost by the month. Many of them are very similar in shape to the original 'Windsurfer' but are probably constructed from different materials. The second generation boards differ not only in shape, but in weight, quality, price and performance.

POINTS TO CONSIDER

First you should decide what the board is to be used for; fooling around on holiday, weekend sailing or racing. You should also decide if it will be used mainly on flat inland water or in open sea.

The size of the sailor will also influence the choice of board. The surface area of the bigger board gives more flotation and is therefore more suitable for heavyweights (70 kilos (154 lbs) — 11 stone or over). The larger board is usually more stable, although not so fast in light winds.

RIGS

The type of rig will also depend on the sailor. A heavy rig with a large sail area is obviously unsuitable for small, light people of either sex. If the board is to be used by all members of the family make sure that the rig is not too heavy for the children, and have a smaller sail available for their use.

Constantly pulling the sail out of the water while learning is the most tiring part, and youngsters can easily be put off if they have been given the wrong rig. Remember to lower the boom to shoulder height for them, or as near as possible.

I have heard people argue that if you learn from the very beginning on a fast 'hairy' board you have a head start. Although this may be true for some sporting types, snow-skiers in particular, it certainly is not always the case. Beginners who do not have good balance become disillusioned and have great trouble just staying on a board which has been designed as a racing machine rather than a learning platform, so find the happy medium: a board which is lively enough to race but is at the same time stable enough to learn on.

CLASSES

The three largest classes in the world are the original 'Windsurfer' — by far the biggest seller worldwide; the 'Windglider'; and the

'Mistral'. They have One-Design Class Associations and are the most serious contenders for the choice of board for the Olympic Games.

MATERIALS

An important factor to look for when choosing your board is the kind of material from which it is made. Four materials are used for making boards at present: polyethylene, fibreglass, A.B.S. plastic, and wood. Polyethylene is perhaps the toughest material. The board can be kicked around without damaging it and is flexible enough to absorb knocks, but when it does get seriously damaged it is difficult to repair. Fibreglass gives a flawless, polished finish and is difficult to beat, but care must be taken not to touch stones or sharp objects as this can easily damage the shell which is fairly brittle. It is, however, by far the easiest material to repair, and this can be done in a matter of minutes on the beach. A.B.S. plastic is a very tough material, capable of absorbing most knocks, and has a long life. Although not the easiest material to repair, it can be done with a special repair kit. Wooden boards must be treated with care as they tend to be made as light as possible and are therefore rather delicate. The quickest way to repair them is with a glass-fibre patch.

KITS

A few specialised companies are now making boards in kit form, which reduces the cost of owning a board, and this is a market which is bound to expand.

One company makes a board which is in sections and can be taken apart, put into a canvas bag the size of a large suitcase and transported anywhere. This is obviously the answer for people without cars or for those who wish to travel to exotic far-away places but still have their own board along with them. This board, incidentally, can be made into a tandem, simply by adding more sections.

Other variations include an 'inflatable', a 'catamaran' and small scale boards for children.

TANDEMS

It is possible to sail on a normal board with two (preferably light-weight) people on it, and this can sometimes help beginners to get an idea of what it is all about, though tacking can be difficult, to say the least! However, if you really want to sample the thrill of high-speed, long-distance surfing with two up, you should try the tandem. This is much longer than the normal board and is equipped with two sails (interchangeable with a single board) and has an enormous dagger-board set between the two masts.

Because of its size and weight it is considerably more stable than the single-sail variety but a whole new set of techniques has to be learnt in order to sail it successfully, and manoeuvring can, literally, cause headaches. Some tandem-surfers wear crash-helmets, and if you have ever seen thirty or forty tandems juggling for position at the start of a race you will know why!

'SAILING' ON THE LAND

New ways of using the 'wishbone' sail are constantly being invented, and these include the 'Wind-Skater', the 'Ice-Surfer', the 'Land-Surfer' and so on.

The Wind-Skater is basically a skateboard with a wishbone rig attached to it. The apparatus can achieve fast speeds on asphalt or other hard ground, but falling can be painful and it is advisable to wear knee and head protection.

The Ice-Surfer achieves speeds of up to 60 mph on frozen lakes or on hard packed snow. It is about five or six feet long and has three skis, similar to a toboggan. The normal rig is then attached using a slot for the mast-foot. The apparatus is manufactured in Germany, but could be built fairly easily by an enterprising amateur.

The Land-Surfer again uses the normal rig, but this time it is attached to a chassis which has pram-type wheels. Great speeds and distances can be achieved (one recently drove down the west coast of Africa) and no doubt a whole set of new records will soon come into being.

Talking of records (back on the water again) a long-distance boardsailing record was set in 1979 of 6 hrs 49 mins for 100 miles, off the coast of Florida. Other records are being set regularly, including the English Channel crossing, and trips across the Straits of Gibraltar, San Francisco Bay, the Bering Straits, and so on.

Several countries, and notably Britain, hold a Speed Week, where records are set by sailing over a set distance (usually 1 kilometre). It is open to every type of sailing craft, providing it is driven only by sail, and the sailboard has amazed everyone by clocking up over 23 knots!

In these days of energy shortages, boardsailing obviously has a great future, for the only energy it uses is yours and the wind's!

Chapter 3

CLOTHING AND EQUIPMENT

The feeling of absolute freedom when sailing in exotic places like the Caribbean, the Seychelles, or the Mediterranean in summertime has to be experienced to be believed. Clothing there consists only of a bathing suit, and falling in becomes a pleasure, or even a necessity in order to cool off! This type of sailing is, unfortunately, only for the lucky ones who live in these areas or for the growing number of people who make their way from Northern Europe to the sunny coasts of the Mediterranean, or further afield, to enjoy boardsailing holidays.

It is very important to be suitably dressed for windsurfing, particularly in the British Isles, where the weather is often far from idyllic. In the right clothing, it is not such a problem to beat the elements and stay warm (if not dry).

On a recent trip to Germany and Holland I was amazed to see at first hand just how incredibly popular the sport has become there, and yet their climate is not so different from the U.K. Every lake, reservoir and gravel pit was crowded with board-sailors in spite of the low temperatures. The majority of the sailors were well prepared for the conditions and wearing full-length neoprene suits to protect themselves from the cold.

WET-SUITS

As a general rule, if the water temperature is below 18°C (62°F) it is advisable to wear a wet-suit to guard against cramp and cold. Suits especially designed for board-sailors and water-skiers (not sub-aqua diving suits) are now available in various styles, sizes and colours. They are light and flexible and do not inhibit movement. Perhaps the best type for use in the U.K. is the full-length 'Long-John' variety which can be worn with or without a bolero-style long-sleeved jacket. The suit should fit closely enough to retain warmth, but not so tightly as to make movement difficult. The thickness of the material varies from 1/16 inch to 3/16 inch; the suit should have neoprene on most of the outside to shed water, thus preventing loss of heat, with nylon on the inside. The zipper must be corrosion-proof and thoroughly stitched into the neoprene material. Make sure the suit is strongly reinforced and that it is not going to tear under the severe stress it will be given, and also that it is suitable for use in salt water. It pays to take care in choosing the right suit for the particular conditions, but the most expensive suit is not necessarily the best. (See Fig. 7.)

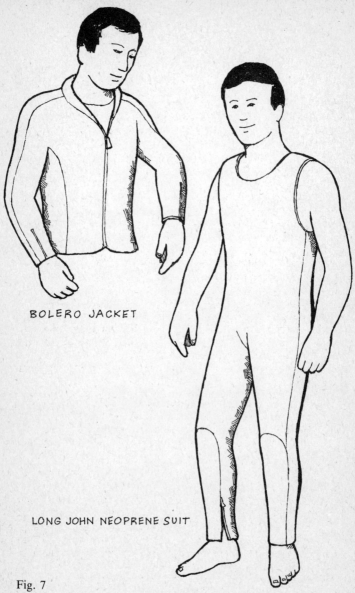

BOLERO JACKET

LONG JOHN NEOPRENE SUIT

Fig. 7

18

LIFEJACKET

A neoprene suit has some buoyancy built in which may help a little in holding someone up in the water, but this is no substitute for a lifejacket, which should be worn in open water, particularly by beginners.

SHOES AND BOOTS

Contact with the board is very important at all times and whether you sail in bare feet, in gym shoes, or windsurfing boots, will depend not only on the state of the weather, but also on the kind of surface the board has. The grip obtained by your feet on the board will differ according to whether the board is made from fibreglass, A.B.S. or polyethylene. It will also vary depending on the type of non-slip design built into the hull; stripes, criss-cross pattern etc. Sun oil, deposited by the sailor, can also reduce grip.

A board made from polyethylene has an excellent surface when new, due to the fine texture, and even when wet gives a good grip to bare feet, but a better grip is obtained when special footwear is used. An A.B.S. board offers a fairly good grip in general, though the surface will vary depending on the manufacturer, so here it is largely a question of personal preference.

Most sailors now use rubber-soled shoes or boots not only to get a surer foothold on the board, but also to protect the feet and ankles from the cold, and from cuts and scratches which might be caused by the mast-foot or daggerboard. It is also preferable to wear something on your feet for comfort and safety when wading in and out of the water as well as while sailing in shallow water, where you might fall and touch the bottom.

Boardsailor's Shin, Sailboarder's Ankle, Windsurfer's Elbow, and so on, are new ailments which have not yet appeared in the medical dictionary!

Special boots are available, made from various materials including neoprene, with flexible 'full-grip' soles of rubber, with padded ankle supports and toes. Make sure that when they have a zipper, it is made from either plastic or other rustproof material, and that the soles are made from thin rubber through which you can feel the board. The boots should be used only for boardsailing as the soles can easily be damaged while walking over stones or sharp objects.

Tennis or running shoes also give a good grip, providing they have rubber soles, not composition or plastic, but it must be noted that these are not designed for use in water. They will probably rot after a short time and will not keep out the cold.

GLOVES

The other essential point of contact with the board is of course the hands and although most sailors feel they obtain a better grip without gloves, it does depend to a certain extent on the type of boom used, and also on the amount of frost around. The original 'Windsurfer' has a wooden boom and the hand-hold is good, though not to everyone's liking, but most modern boards are equipped with aluminium booms with various types of covering, or even no covering at all. Most sailors who wear gloves do so not only against the cold, but also to avoid blisters and cramp.

SPARE CLOTHING

Warm, dry clothing should be on hand after sailing, particularly thick woollen socks, dry shoes, a sweater and a large towel.

SPECTACLES

A word about spectacles. It can be dangerous to wear glass-lensed spectacles while boardsailing. Plastic lenses are better but far from ideal. Frames are available made specially for athletes, which fit right around the ear, or have a notch for an elastic band. The real answer is to wear contact lenses which have been designed for water sports.

ROOF RACKS

A roof rack is an essential piece of equipment if you are to transport the board any distance by car. There are specially designed racks for transporting your board, and they vary in price and quality. The rack should be built to withstand a weight of at least 80 lbs, rustproof, easy to put on and off, preferably lockable (boards are easily stolen) and with a separate fastening for the mast. When loading the board on to the roof rack, remember that the bow (front) of the board should always be facing downwards over the front of the car. The board, or boards (it is possible to carry two or more if you have a suitable rack) should be fixed securely with rope, but **not** stretch 'spiders', as the board tends to lift at speed. Make sure the rack is attached securely, and don't drive too fast. If the mast hangs out over the back of the car, tie a white rag to it, and affix a red light at night. (See Fig. 8.)

   Unless it is a very short journey, when the sail can be rolled around the mast after detaching the boom, it is best to take the sail off the mast completely and stow it in a sail-bag in the boot of the car, along with the daggerboard.

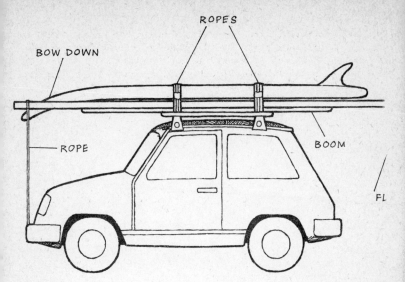

Fig. 8

TOOLS

It is always a good idea to take along some spare line of various thicknesses, adhesive tape, a screwdriver and a pair of pliers for doing the odd repair job. A box of matches or cigarette lighter might also come in handy, not for seeing which way the wind is blowing, but for burning the end of synthetic line to stop it from fraying.

While it would hardly be regarded by most people as essential equipment, there is a growing industry making T-shirts, shorts, sweaters, caps, bags, etc. — you name it — with the word 'Windsurfing', 'Surf', 'Boardsailing' and other symbols, designs and brand-names printed or stitched on them. These articles could perhaps be described as 'Après-Surf' kit, and if you feel that way inclined, why not?

Chapter 4

PREPARING THE BOARD AND THE SAILOR

Let us suppose that you have a brand-new board and you want to put
it together.

Fig. 9

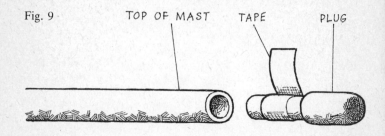

TOP OF MAST   TAPE   PLUG

The mast should have a small piece of wood or plastic pushed into
the top of it to seal the end, and to keep the water out. Some makes of
board have this small but important item mixed up in the bag of
tricks along with ropes, sail, daggerboard, mast-foot etc., so make
sure you find it and plug it into the top of the mast, wrapping a little
tape around it if necessary to make a tight fit. The type of mast-foot
will vary, depending on the make of board, but whatever the type, the
stock should be allowed to revolve freely inside the mast. Check it
from time to time after use, especially the wooden type which might
expand when wet, making it difficult to take out. Water inside the
mast makes it heavy. (See Fig. 9.)

The universal joint should also be looked at regularly, whatever
type it is, as this is a very important piece of equipment, constantly in
motion while sailing, and subject to wear.

Having plugged the top of the mast, slot the sleeve of the sail over it
and pull it gently down. The small line attached to the mast-foot,
which should have a 'bowline' tied in it, should then be threaded
through the metal hole at the bottom of the sail and tightened until
the mast bends just a little.

THE BOOM

To attach the boom to the mast, first find the required height by
standing the mast up straight with the mast-foot in the sand or loose
ground, and mark your shoulder height on the mast with a pencil.
Then, in the space indicated on the mast at about shoulder level, tie a
'rolling-hitch', making it very tight. The boom is supported only by

this knot, except in the case of some more recent boards which have a plastic or metal boom-attachment. Pass the line through a cleat on the boom and tighten it until the mast is touching **the inside front of the boom**. The 'outhaul' line at the other end of the boom should then be threaded through the hole in the sail and tightened to the required tension.

The degree to which you tighten the sail will depend on the amount of wind there is. For example, in light wind the sail should have full 'belly', whereas in stronger wind it should be 'flattened', by tightening the outhaul and downhaul. The uphaul line should be passed through a hole in the attachment at the front of the boom and a normal knot tied in it to stop it from being pulled through. Once in place, tie two or three other knots at intervals of about eight or nine inches to provide a good hand-grip. The elastic line should be attached to the uphaul line about a foot from the bottom, and the plastic clip attached loosely to the downhaul line under the sail. The uphaul line should be fairly slack so that it can be grabbed from any angle easily, but not so slack that you might trip over it.

BATTENS

Lastly, the three sail-battens (if the sail requires them) should be slotted carefully into place. The rig is now complete.

The board has only one permanent attachment, and that is the small fin or 'skeg' which is usually screwed onto the underside of the board. Use a little silicone or putty in the screw-holes to stop water seeping in.

Always carry the rig above your head with the mast-foot facing the wind and lay the rig (mast, boom and sail together) on the water first, **always** before the board. The sail acts as an anchor, so the rig will not go very far, but the board on its own will quickly drift away, downwind, so it cannot be left. Carry the board to the water, the fingers of the left hand in the mast-step slot, the fingers of the right hand in the daggerboard case from the other side (see Fig. 10).

Push the daggerboard down (the right way round, sloping backwards), and then ease the mast-foot into position. It should be a firm fit but not so tight that it cannot slip out in an emergency. Be careful of the daggerboard in shallow water. The most common damage done to a board is caused by forgetting to lift the daggerboard when coming into shallow water, then hitting a rock or stone and forcing the daggerboard sharply backwards, damaging the rear of the daggerboard case.

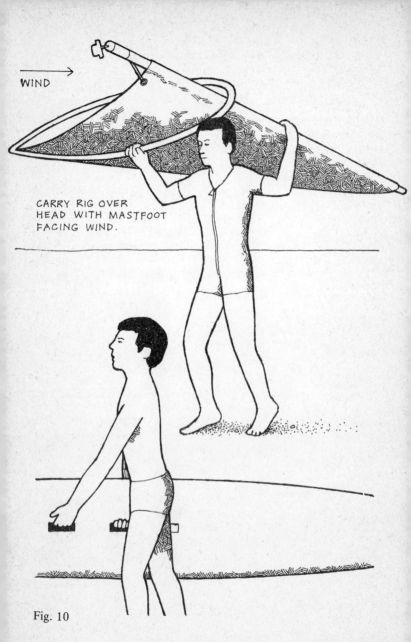

WIND →

CARRY RIG OVER
HEAD WITH MASTFOOT
FACING WIND.

Fig. 10

KNOTS

The more knots you know how to tie, and to untie, the better; but there are three essential ones for the windsurfer. It is important to have the right kind of line or rope, and although this is normally supplied it is not always adequate for the job.

The Rolling Hitch is the important knot, tied around the mast and used for holding the boom in position. It should be practised first on the mast without the sail, and later with the sail in place. The line should be of good quality, soft yet strong, and generous in length, but not made from nylon, which is inclined to slip and stretch. (See Fig. 11.)

The Bowline is a much-used knot, well known to any sailor. On the original Windsurfer it is used for tying the wooden booms together at the back. It is also used, on most boards, on the luff downhaul line to keep the front (luff) of the sail taut. (See Fig. 12.)

The Reef Knot and the *Half-Hitch* are both simple and useful knots which are easy to make in a hurry. (See Fig. 12.)

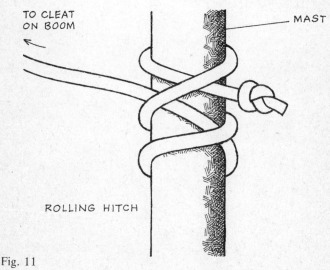

TO CLEAT ON BOOM

MAST

ROLLING HITCH

Fig. 11

BOWLINE

REEF KNOT

Fig. 12

GETTING FIT

Many people learning boardsailing will no doubt have some experience of dinghy sailing, and probably think that this new sport is not really so new, but just a variation on a theme. They're in for a big surprise! Although it may be of some advantage to them when they become more advanced and can use the wind (in races for example), the basic technique is very different and has to be learnt from scratch.

There are others who think it is a sport only for 'he-men' and that you have to be some kind of Superman (or crazy) even to attempt it. Well, there is no doubt that if you want to go boardsailing for any length of time in a strong breeze, you must be fit, and if you intend to sail in regattas, very fit, but there are hundreds and thousands of small, slender, boys and girls enjoying the sport who bear no resemblance to Mr. Universe! My guide for children is simple: if they are strong enough to haul the sail out of the water, they can handle the board.

26

PULL-UPS

JACKNIFE

PRESS-UPS

Fig. 13

27

Some simple exercises to help get you in condition should include the following (see Fig. 13):

Pull-ups on a horizontal bar.

Press-ups on the floor.

Tug-of-War or rope pulling, if you don't have an opponent.

Jacknife — lying on the floor, raising your legs and back.

Warming-up before sailing is very advisable, even in warmer climates, so that the muscles function efficiently. Jogging, skipping or making short sprints will do the trick.

If you have access to a gymnasium, all the better. Exercises on wall-bars are particularly beneficial for tuning-up muscles, but remember that the muscles which take most of the strain are in the forearms, hands and shoulders, although in boardsailing you use almost every muscle in the body.

Practically any form of exercise is good for getting in condition for boardsailing, particularly trampolining, tennis, swimming, squash etc., and I know some sailors who take a small, hard, rubber ball with them to the office, and squeeze it in the palm of the hand in order to strengthen their grip. Balance, rather than weight and strength, is the key to boardsailing, and it is significant that many alpine, downhill skiers make very good board-sailors.

Chapter 5

FIRST STEPS IN BOARDSAILING

For your first attempt, choose a very calm day with flat water and just a breath of wind. If you are able to practise on a dry-land simulator, preferably with a qualified instructor to guide you, then take advantage of it. However, I will assume that you are attempting to teach yourself how to windsurf with just the help of this book.

The board has been rigged correctly and is lying in waist-deep water with the daggerboard down. Find the wind direction by watching flags, chimney-smoke etc., and place the sail on the **opposite** side of the board to the wind.

FINDING THE WIND

Climbing on to the board in shallow water should present no problem. First kneel down over the daggerboard case and then get up slowly, placing one foot either side of the mast while facing the sail. Stay in this position for a while, get used to being on the water, and try transferring your weight from one foot to the other and from the heel to the toe. Once you find your balance, and only then, keeping one foot each side of the mast on the imaginary 'centre-line' of the board, crouch down, knees to the chest, and take hold of the uphaul line. Pull hard at first, using all your weight, until the top of the mast comes clear of the water. Once out of the water the sail will come up quickly and as it does so you should try to get your hands to the top of the uphaul line as soon as possible, and at the same time straighten up your back until your legs and trunk are in a straight line.

Now, hold the mast in line with your body, directly in front of you, the tip of the boom just clear of the water and the sail held at right angles to the board. In this way you automatically find the direction of the wind. Remember that the sail will rest at **90 degrees** to the board, and the wind will come from your back. (See Fig. 14.)

MOVING OFF

With one hand now at the top of the uphaul line, and the arm slightly bent, try gently moving the rig (mast, sail and boom) backwards and forwards. You will notice that a small amount of movement is enough to turn this board one way or the other. Take your time, get used to being 'on board' and try to relax.

If you are making your first attempt in open water it is advisable to have the board attached with a line through the daggerboardcase to a concrete block or sand-filled rubber tyre on the sea bed. It should be long enough to allow freedom of movement and preferably have

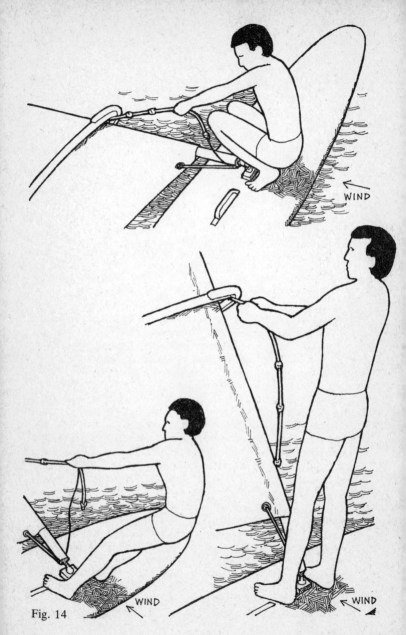

Fig. 14

an elastic shock-cord to avoid sudden jolts. In this way you can practise all the movements and positions of sail, without the danger of drifting off-shore.

If you have helpers with you, make sure they stand well away from the board, as holding the board, or worse still, holding the end of the boom, does not help the beginner at all. On the contrary, it is a hindrance as the board should be allowed to swing freely so that the effect of changing the position of the mast will be felt quickly.

You will no doubt by now have noticed what a sensitive piece of equipment the sailboard is, and how quickly it will turn, usually towards the wind. Balancing becomes more difficult when there are small waves which rock the board, so keep your feet in the middle of the board and transfer your weight evenly from heel to toe. Do not worry about falling in, for everyone does. It is much easier to fall off than to climb back on — it is climbing back which makes you tired! Just try to analyse what went wrong and slowly get back into the starting position. Once there, standing with your feet straddling the mast, prepare once more for take-off!

BASIC POSITION

You are standing up straight, your back to the wind, sail at right angles to the board, hand at the top of the uphaul line, and you want to get yourself in the position to sail forwards.

Let us say that you have the front of the board facing right, in the direction you wish to sail. Place your right foot (now called the front foot) next to the mast, and the left foot (the back foot) just in front of the daggerboard case. Holding the top of the uphaul line with the left hand, cross the right hand over to grasp the boom about 9 inches back from the mast. Once you have a firm grip, let the uphaul line fall (you do not need it for a while) and hold the sail in this position, just clear of the water, still at 90 degrees to the board. (See Fig. 15.) Now pull the rig towards you **across** the board, past the shoulder, and at the same time lean the top of the mast **forwards**, over the bow. Only when you have the rig in this position should you reach out and take the boom with the left hand (now known as the sail hand) and pull the sail in towards you. As you pull the rig towards you, some pressure will be felt on the sail because you are presenting the whole area of sail to the wind and the more wind there is, the more you need to compensate by leaning your weight against the wind. (See Fig. 16.)

Your arms should be bent, with your elbows down at the sides of your body in order to keep the boom as close to the body as possible and to keep the rig as vertical as you can. Your back should always be kept straight or slightly arched, with your shoulders back. You should try never to lean forwards towards the sail. Once the sail escapes and

31

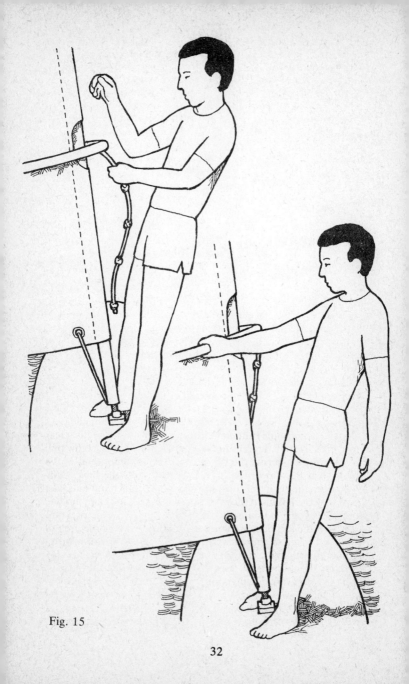

Fig. 15

1. PULL RIG IN, <u>PAST</u> THE SHOULDER.

2. LEAN MAST OVER AND FORWARDS THEN TAKE BOOM AND PULL IT TOWARDS YOU SLOWLY.

3. BACK STRAIGHT, KEEP THE BOOM CLOSE TO YOU, MAST LEANING SLIGHTLY FORWARDS.

Fig. 16

33

the force of the wind on it pulls you forwards to leeward, and your back becomes bent past the point of no return, drop the sail and start again.

Start again by taking the top of the uphaul line and getting into the start position once more. Let us go over that once again because it is extremely important to get it right:

1. Take the uphaul line in the left hand, the sail at 90 degrees to the board, wind at your back.
2. Cross the right hand over onto the boom; let go of the line.
3. Pull the rig towards you, across the imaginary centre-line of the board, and lean it forwards to avoid turning into the wind.
4. Move the left (back) foot to a position over the daggerboard case and at the same time pull the boom towards you with the left (sail) hand.
5. Face the front of the board and, still with the mast leaning forwards, put more weight on the back foot and lean out, against the wind.

When the board is facing in the other direction everything will be reversed, so that the left hand will become the mast-hand while the right hand becomes the sail-hand. Similarly, the left foot becomes the front foot and so on . . .

By this time you will probably have lost your balance and fallen in a few times! Try not to let it discourage you — it is quite normal and happens to every beginner. You should, however, be able to make some progress in a forward direction by now. If you are not getting anywhere, go over the basic points once again, for there is something you haven't got quite right. Practise a while in light winds, feel the effect the wind has on the sail when it is pulled in, how it propels the board forwards, even in very light winds. Stay close to the shore, though; you have not yet learnt how to turn around and sail back!

TURNING

The most common way of turning the board around is to 'tack' or 'go about' by facing the front of the board towards the wind, at the same time passing the sail from one side to the other over the back of the board. Remember, you should always be on the same side of the board **as the wind**, so to 'tack' you must move from one side of the board to the other by **walking** around the front of the mast (that's all!) always with **your back to the wind**.

Assuming that you are sailing along in the normal way, close-hauled (about 45 degrees off the wind) and you wish to turn the board around and sail the other way, first lean the mast towards the back of the board so that the tip of the boom is almost in the water behind the board. When you do this you will find that the board turns quickly towards the wind. As it does so, take hold of the top of the uphaul line

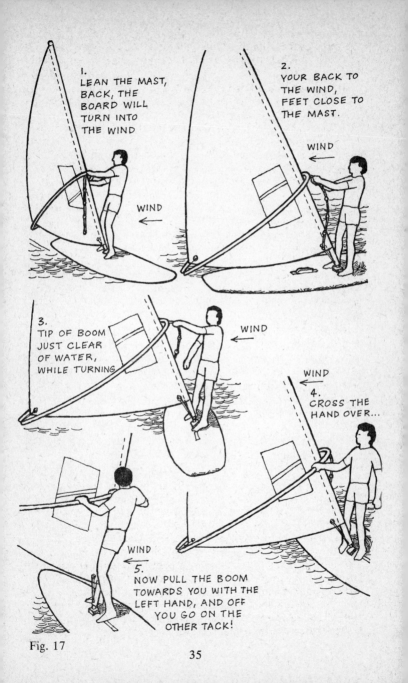

1. LEAN THE MAST, BACK, THE BOARD WILL TURN INTO THE WIND

2. YOUR BACK TO THE WIND, FEET CLOSE TO THE MAST.

WIND

3. TIP OF BOOM JUST CLEAR OF WATER, WHILE TURNING

WIND

4. CROSS THE HAND OVER...

WIND

5. NOW PULL THE BOOM TOWARDS YOU WITH THE LEFT HAND, AND OFF YOU GO ON THE OTHER TACK!

WIND

Fig. 17

35

and let go of the boom. Now, walk gradually around the front of the mast, facing the back of the board, making small steps around the mast, with your feet always in contact with it. Use your free hand for balance, but neither hand should be on the boom while you make this manoeuvre. Make sure that once the board has turned around, you again get the sail at right angles to the board in order to find the wind direction before you prepare to sail off. (See Fig. 17.)

Then follow the starting procedure once more, but this time holding the uphaul line with the right hand, crossing the left hand over and on to the boom, and pulling the sail in with the right hand. The left foot should now be just in front of the mast, while the right foot is now placed over the daggerboard case.

Try sailing up and down like this for a while, practising the 'tack' turning procedure, the wind first on one side, then the other. It will require a lot of concentration, but providing the conditions are right (very light wind and flat water) you should be able to master it — perhaps with a few duckings, but that is perfectly normal. When you fall, by the way, try to fall *away* from the board, not on top of the mast or sail. When you feel tired, give it a break for a while, or try another day. Learning can be hard work, so don't expect too much the first few times.

UNDERSTANDING THE WIND

A source of much confusion to many people who have never sailed before (and to many who have) is the 'feeling' for the wind. Some people have a natural awareness of the wind while others have little or none at all. Most sailors need instruction and practice to use the wind to their advantage.

To the board-sailor the wind is of paramount importance. You should be able to tell at a glance the wind's direction, its strength and whether it is constant or changing speed and direction, before you even go on the water. The practised board-sailor will be able to use wind-shifts to his advantage and will be prepared for any sudden change in the wind's direction.

ON-SHORE AND OFF-SHORE WINDS

Apart from the wind strength or force, there are two kinds of wind the board-sailor should take note of: On-Shore and Off-Shore. The On-Shore wind is no real problem, except if you are sailing on open sea, where it can build up waves or surf. The Off-Shore wind, on the other hand, blowing from the land towards the water, leaves the water flat, but is usually very gusty and unreliable, leaving patches of strong wind in some areas while other areas are protected in the shadow of trees or houses.

A. OFF SHORE WIND. FLAT WATER NEAR COAST. GUSTS OF WIND.

B. ON SHORE WIND. REGULAR WIND. MORE WAVES.

Fig. 18

The On-Shore wind, although creating rougher water, is generally much safer than the Off-Shore wind, for it will blow the surfer ashore if he tires or gets into difficulties. The Off-Shore wind appears to create calm, but it can be dangerous for the beginner as he can drift away from the shore without realising it; he may then find the wind stronger as he gets further out, and sometimes he cannot sail back. Bearing this in mind it is essential that the board-sailor should know what to do in a case like this. Tired and in difficulty in an Off-Shore wind, the drill is to wrap up the sail, lay the rig on the board, and paddle back to shore. (See Fig. 18.)

WIND FORCE

The inexperienced board-sailor should never venture out on the water when the wind is blowing more than *Force 3 Beaufort Scale*. The *Beaufort Scale* is an internationally recognised method of measuring wind strength, and is used for shipping forecasts. The wind speed is difficult to assess from the shore, but the experienced eye will be able to tell roughly the force of the wind by looking at the state of the surface of the sea, as well as feeling the wind in his face. A general guide for the board-sailor goes like this:

Force 0 = Flat calm. No movement on water. (Practise balancing on board without the rig.)

Force 1 = Slight ripples appear. (Beginner's first try.)

Force 2 = Wavelets appear. (Ideal beginner's practice time.)

Force 3 = Small waves with occasional whitecaps. (Good little breeze, sailor beginning to lean out against wind.)

Force 4 = Wave-crests break more frequently. (Ideal racing weather.)

Force 5 = Larger waves with bigger breakers. (Time for an 'All-round' sail.)

Force 6 = Strong wind, troughs, white breakers. (All-round sailing, only for experts.)

Force 7 = Very strong. (Only for the very experienced. Stormsail.)

Force 8 = Gale. (Only for the very experienced. Stormsail.)

Force 9 = Severe Gale. (No sailing today.)

Force 10 = Storm. (No sailing today.)

As you see, it is possible to boardsail in winds where it would be impossible to put to sea in a sailing dinghy. This is because the effective sail area is reduced when the sail leans **towards** the wind. The area of sail actually presented to the wind becomes smaller as the wind becomes stronger and the sailor leans further and further to windward. When the sailor is under the sail like this he has to support some of his own weight and the sail begins to give 'lift', like a kite. This, combined with the lessening of weight on the board, allows the board-sailor to achieve incredible speeds.

It is not possible to reef down the sail on a sailboard, but in winds over Force 5 a smaller '*All-round*' sail would possibly be used and in really strong winds a '*Stormsail*' would be necessary. Sailing for any length of time in strong winds calls for a lot of effort and a great degree of physical fitness.

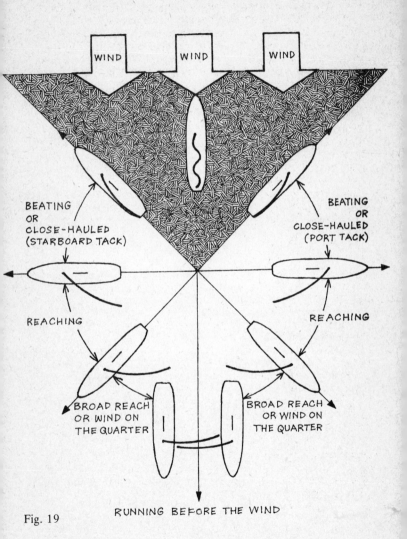

WIND   WIND   WIND

BEATING
OR
CLOSE-HAULED
(STARBOARD TACK)

BEATING
OR
CLOSE-HAULED
(PORT TACK)

REACHING   REACHING

BROAD REACH
OR WIND ON
THE QUARTER

BROAD REACH
OR WIND ON
THE QUARTER

RUNNING BEFORE THE WIND

Fig. 19

Chapter 6

POINTS OF SAILING

Boardsailing, like other forms of sailing, has three basic definitions relating the direction the craft is sailing in to the direction of the wind:

1　Beating
2　Reaching
3　Running

It is essential to know just what these sailing terms mean.

BEATING

Beating to Windward, otherwise known as 'Sailing Close-Hauled', means sailing towards a given point **against the wind direction** by tacking (or zig-zagging) and sailing as close to the wind as possible. It is, of course, impossible to sail directly into the wind, but a good board-sailor can sail at an angle of 40 degrees or less to the wind on either tack. To do this, the mast should be almost vertical and the sail should be pulled right in, to a position over the **centre-line** of the board, but not past it.

The sailor should have his back straight or slightly arched, the arms bent so as to keep the boom as close to him as possible. By leaning the mast back slightly the board will *luff up* to the wind and the sail will start to flap at the leading edge (luff) next to the mast. When this happens it is time to 'bear away' by leaning the mast forward, thus turning the board away from the wind. There is an art in sailing well to windward and it is usually on this 'leg' that a race is won or lost.

Foot Positions are very important and will vary depending on the wind strength. In light winds the feet should be close together to concentrate the weight just behind the mast, while in stronger winds the weight should be moved further aft, with the front leg braced against the mast and the back leg behind the daggerboard case (see Fig. 20). In very strong winds and in surf, the back foot should be moved to the edge of the board to stop it from flipping over.

In order to *beat to windward* in strong winds you will need to move the centre of gravity out further by 'hanging' under the boom and using your own weight to counterbalance the wind strength.

Fig. 20

BEATING

When beating, the wind will push the board sideways, especially in light airs. Against this we have only two weapons, firstly the dagger-board, which should always be fully down when beating, and secondly, in stronger winds, tilting the board slightly to stop it sliding sideways, by placing the feet nearer the edge. *Beating to windward* in, say, Force 4 or more is, let's face it, hard work. The board-sailor has to be fit and have strong arms and hands. The fingers and hands should be moved slightly from time to time, changing from the normal 'over-grip' — with the knuckles upwards — to the 'under-grip' with the knuckles down, or perhaps an alternate grip — one grip for one hand, and one for the other. (See Fig. 21.)

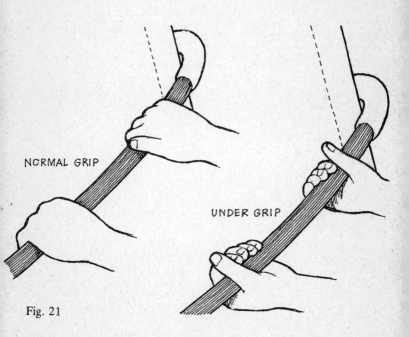

NORMAL GRIP

UNDER GRIP

Fig. 21

REACHING

This is the fastest point of sailing, when the wind is on the side of the board and the sail is let out a little.

Even to get into this position can cause difficulties. Bearing *off the wind*, particularly in stronger winds, is not easy, and almost everyone learning boardsailing has trouble with it.

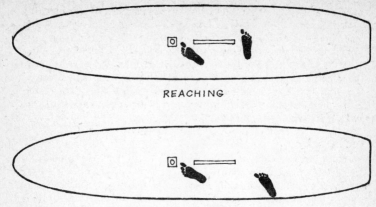

REACHING

REACHING IN STRONG WIND

Fig. 22

Imagine that you are sailing close-hauled and you want to turn away from the wind (*bear off*). Firstly, lean the top of the mast forwards, still keeping the **pressure on the sail**. The board will start to '*bear away*'; move your hands further back along the boom and in this way you will keep the mast leaning forwards and to windward, while keeping the weight towards the back of the board. Try to keep the centre of gravity low by bending the knees, until you have completed the manoeuvre and the board is facing in the direction you want to sail. Then:

1. Let the sail out with the sail hand.
2. Brace your front foot against the mast-step.
3. Put your back foot behind the daggerboard case.
4. Bend the back leg to move your centre of gravity further back. (See Fig. 22.)

Sailing with the wind on the beam (beam = side), or 'reaching' as it is more commonly called, is when you have the wind more or less on the side of the board, which often means a Beam Sea — waves hitting the side of the board, making it more unstable than usual — so your reactions have to be rather fast. Study the 'Points of Sailing' diagram again (Fig. 19).

A *Broad Reach* is the term used for the point of sailing when the wind is further round towards the **back** of the board, though not yet directly behind it. Here you should keep your weight even further back and either lift up the daggerboard about half way or hinge it back (depending on the type) to achieve maximum speed. With a good wind the board will begin to 'plane' almost immediately on the

42

smallest of waves, and achieve fast speeds. The first few times this occurs the surfer is often so amazed at the speed at which he is travelling that he just falls off!

The tendency is for the sailor to be catapulted over the front of the board, and to avoid this the centre of gravity must be kept low over the back of the board by bracing the front foot against the bottom of the mast and fully bending the back leg, transferring most of the weight to it and at the same time pulling downwards with the sail hand and getting under the sail.

RUNNING

Running, or sailing 'before the wind', is the term used to describe the position of sailing with the wind directly behind the board. This is the most unstable position in which to sail and the most difficult to master, particularly in strong winds. The sail should now be at right angles to the board, and, at the same time, the mast should be leaned to the left or to the right over the board in order to steer it. The sailor should be facing the front of the board, with one foot on each side, just behind the daggerboard case, back straight, arms and legs slightly bent (see Figs. 23 and 24). In light winds the mast will be vertical (seen from the side), but in stronger winds the mast should be leaned backwards and your weight moved further aft, the legs bent a little more and the shoulders back. To reduce the area of sail presented to the wind the sail should be pulled in as well as leaned backwards.

The instability experienced when sailing before the wind is due to the fact that you no longer have any 'lateral resistance' to the wind — in other words, nothing to 'hang' on. It will become easier with practice.

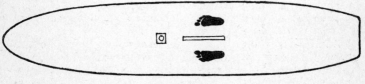

Fig. 23   RUNNING

These three 'points of sailing' are fundamental in boardsailing. With them the sailor can make the board go in the required direction, and not just where the wind wills it. Now let us look at some refinements.

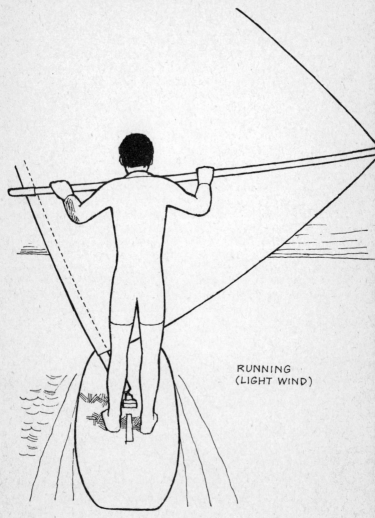

RUNNING
(LIGHT WIND)

Fig. 24

Chapter 7

JET-TACKING, GYBING, MANOEUVRING

It is possible to 'tack' a sailboard very quickly and within a very small area. It will turn literally in its own length, and when sailed by an expert will tack faster than a sailing dinghy. With the dinghy the skipper and his crew have to duck under the boom when going about (or gybing), but the board-sailor, when tacking, has to walk his way around the **front** of the mast.

TACKING

Tacking, or 'going about', means turning the front of the board through the eye of the wind and so changing the sail from one side of the board to the other. To turn the board into the wind, assuming you are sailing 'close-hauled' at 40 or 45 degrees to the wind — first lean the mast back until the end of the boom is almost in the water behind the board; the front edge (luff) of the sail will begin to flap as you 'luff up' into the wind. Secondly, take hold of the 'uphaul line' (near the mast) and move gently around the front of the mast, keeping the feet close to the mast (see Fig. 25). Thirdly, crossing the hands over, pull the boom in towards you, leaning the mast forwards at the same time until you gather speed; then gradually ease the mast back to its normal 'beating' position (almost vertical, slightly forward).

This manoeuvre must be practised **over and over again** until you are able to do it very quickly.

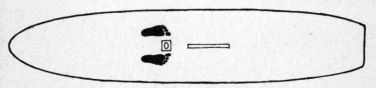

Fig. 25   GOING ABOUT

THE JET-TACK

When you are more experienced you could try what is known as a 'Jet-Tack' where the board is forced to turn through the wind by pulling the sail across the board, at the same time as leaning the mast back. All your weight is put momentarily on the back foot. In the exact moment that the front of the board passes through the wind, you literally 'jump' around the mast, grab the boom on the other side and sail off on the other tack. The idea is to keep the sail full of wind all the time and not lose valuable time turning around with the board facing the wind and the sail not working.

GYBING

Gybing means changing the sail from one side of the board to the other in order to sail off in a different direction, this time with the **back** of the board facing the wind.

Board-sailors can do this by letting the sail swing around the front of the board, unlike the dinghy helmsman, who lets it swing around the stern and must again duck under the boom.

To gybe, firstly, you must get yourself into the 'running' position, sailing with the wind directly behind you with the sail out at right angles to the board. Let us assume that you have been 'bearing away' from the wind (by leaning the mast well forward) and now have the sail out on the right side of the board, and you wish to turn further to the right. The back of the board can go a little way past the wind, still with the sail on this side (known as 'sailing by the lee'), but there comes a point where the sail must be swung around the other side if you want to go further to the right. Standing well back, move the right foot to a point just behind the mast and at the same time lean the mast across to the left of the board. Then let go of the boom with the right ('sail') hand and allow the boom to swing horizontally around the **front** of the board, while holding the top of the 'uphaul' line with the left hand. The right hand has now become the 'mast-hand', having crossed over the top to grasp the boom, and you are now able (I hope) to pull the sail with your left hand acting as the sail hand, and sail away merrily on a reach. The same procedure would of course apply on the other tack, but with everything reversed. (See Fig. 26.)

An important thing to remember is to change your foot position **before** gybing, and to execute the manoeuvre as smoothly and as quickly as possible. Gybing becomes difficult, if not downright impossible, in strong winds.

MANOEUVRING WITH THE MAST

As you have seen, steering the board is done mainly by the movement of the mast, leaning it towards the front of the board or to the back, or from side to side (see Fig. 27.).

Moving it forward or backward changes the centre of effort on the sail to a position further forward or further aft in relation to the board. At the same time your weight should be transferred forward or backward along the board in order to help it turn and also to

Fig. 26

47

BEAR AWAY.
MAST FORWARDS.

LUFF UP.
MAST BACK.

Fig. 27

compensate for the pressure on the sail and to keep the board as level as possible. Always keep some pressure on the sail when attempting to 'bear away' from the wind until the board is sailing on the course you have chosen; only then should you let the sail out and take full advantage of the wind.

Practise sailing a 'wavy' course, alternately 'luffing up' and 'bearing away', and you will notice how a very small movement of the mast will change the course of the board. Who needs a rudder?

STOPPING

If you need to stop the board in a hurry, the best way is to throw the rig in the water, jump in yourself, and hold the sail. I am assuming that the mast-foot is attached to the board (the two should never be allowed to drift apart). This is without doubt the surest way of coming to a halt, particularly in a strong wind. The more experienced sailor would probably 'back' the sail, getting the wind on the 'wrong' side, which acts as a brake. If in doubt, or to avoid a collision, drop the sail or simply let go of the boom and take hold of the uphaul line, letting the sail swing free. Then sit on the board until you can sail on.

Chapter 8

SAILING IN STRONG WINDS

When you have become sufficiently competent and confident to sail in about wind strength 3 (Beaufort) then, **and only then,** should you try boardsailing in stronger winds.

This involves learning new techniques, and you will probably spend quite a lot of time in the water until you get the hang of it, and 'hang' is the operative word. This is the secret of sailing in strong wind — literally 'hanging on the wind', feeling the sail lift and the board plane at great speed.

It is here that the so called 'Apparent Wind' becomes increasingly important. This is not the true direction of the wind. The Apparent Wind is the combination of the board's own forward motion, which in itself causes wind, *plus* the wind on the side of the sail becoming 'bent' the faster you travel forwards. (See Fig. 28.)

The sail should be made flatter by pulling the 'outhaul' line as well as the luff-downhaul line together. The mast will then be bent and the sail will have far less 'belly' than in lighter winds. You can practise this ashore by pushing the mast-foot into the sand and holding the boom

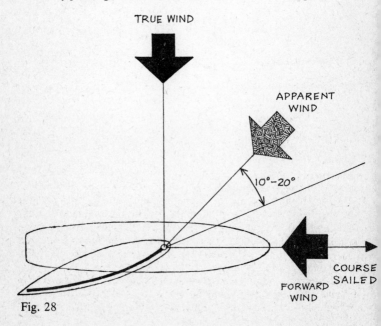

Fig. 28

as if you were out sailing, to test the shape of the sail with a strong wind on it. 'Hanging out' requires quite a lot of skill and practice, as well as quick reactions. The foot position will change with the conditions and the body must flex continually in order to compensate for the wind and waves. You will never be closer to nature than this! Every little change in the wind direction or strength, in wave pattern or surf, will be felt by the sailor and he or she must know how to react instinctively.

Fig. 29

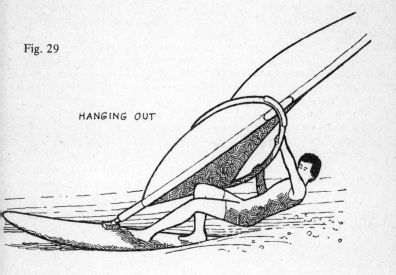

HANGING OUT

BODY-DIPS

When the sail is pulled in tight (sheeted in) the sailor must lean all, or most of his weight **against** the wind. The more the wind tries to pull you over to leeward, the more you must counteract it by leaning outwards and 'under' the sail until the body is almost horizontal, the shoulders very close to the sea (see Fig. 29). Some surfers lean so far out that their body touches the water and even the head goes under! Known as a 'body-dip' or 'head-dip', it looks spectacular and is great fun though it is mainly done for show.

When sailing in fairly strong winds and 'hanging out', the centre of gravity is moved outwards and the mast leans over the water. Steering becomes more difficult, although it is still done by leaning the top of

51

the mast back to 'luff up' and forward to 'bear away'. You will find that a very small change of angle is sufficient to change your course, providing that you keep pressure on the sail by leaning out and at the same time pulling in with the 'sail' hand. It is always a good idea to have company when sailing, particularly in strong winds, and it is in this way that you learn to steer, by following one another in a snake formation, luffing up and bearing away, comparing your own position and performance, preferably with someone who has more experience than yourself.

PRACTICE

Build up gradually to sail in stronger winds, preferably without the big sea which accompanies them when sailing in open water with an on-shore wind. Perhaps the best place to practise sailing in strong winds the first few times is on a lake, where the wind is unlikely to build up large waves. Trying to cope with both wind and waves is confusing; it is best to master one thing at a time. When travelling fast keep the centre of gravity low, brace the front foot against the back of the mast-foot, keep the front leg straight while bending the back leg, and keep the back foot well behind the daggerboard case. Sailing downwind in these conditions requires good balance and co-ordination, with the feet well back behind the daggerboard case and the whole rig leaning backwards. Your weight must be used to keep the board as level as possible, so the more pressure there is on the sail, forcing the bow downwards, the more it must be counteracted by placing your weight further aft. When 'running' before the wind or sometimes on a 'reach', the daggerboard can be either raised or removed completely to reduce friction. Taking it out completely is quite a difficult operation in strong wind, requiring very good balance, as the board becomes very unstable. One hand must reach down to pull the daggerboard out, while the other must hold the whole rig. It is a risky thing to do in a race, where on the downwind section you could gain quite a lot by sailing faster without the daggerboard (hanging it on your arm) but on the other hand you could lose a few places if you take a fall.

PROBLEMS

Starting in a strong wind almost always causes difficulties. Most beginners have the same fault; they are afraid to lean the mast far enough over to begin with and consequently the wind pulls them to leeward right away. The knack is to lean the mast well over to windward and at the same time forward, **before** taking hold of the boom. Then when you grab the boom, lean your weight out immediately in order to keep the centre of gravity low down. The more wind there is, the more you must lean the mast. Providing there is enough wind, it is even possible to do a 'water start' by heaving yourself out of the water rather like a water-skier, just using pressure of the wind on the sail, but you are going to need a lot of practice to get to this stage.

Beating to windward, or sailing on a 'reach' in a strong wind, requires the sailor to hang out almost horizontally **under** the sail supporting much of his own weight in the process. This action, unique to boardsailing, uses the sail not only for forward propulsion but also to give 'lift' like an aerofoil. The more wind there is, the more the sailor hangs out, pulling downwards on the sail. This reduces the weight he puts on the board, which, being so light, planes even more easily and achieves high speeds. When this happens the board becomes more unstable than usual and the back foot has sometimes to be pushed hard down on the edge of the board to stop it from flipping over. Sailing in these conditions is very tiring, but very exciting.

WORD OF WARNING

Don't get so carried away with the thrill of travelling at great speeds that you forget your whereabouts. Check your position regularly and make sure that you do not go too far away from the shore. In a strong wind you will become tired after a short time, especially if you fall a lot, and it will require all your strength to sail back to the shore. If you find that you are unable to sail back to the point of departure, because you have drifted down the coast and can't *beat to windward* any more, try to sail on a 'reach' towards the coast. If this fails, either because you are too exhausted, or because there is too much wind, take hold of the top of the uphaul line and let the end of the boom trail in the water so that the wind partly fills the sail. This will be sufficient to propel you fairly quickly without too much effort and without having your hands on the boom, steering by leaning the mast one way or the other.

THE HARNESS OR TRAPEZE

When you have become fairly proficient at boardsailing and wish to sail for longer periods, one solution is to wear a harness. This will enable you to sail to windward without so much strain on the arms and hands as it supports you with an attachment to the boom from the harness worn around your chest or waist.

Various types are available and it is really a question of individual preference. There are arguments for and against wearing harnesses in races, and these can only be decided by the Race Committee.

Chapter 9

SAILING IN SURF AND WAVES

Sailing in surf or in big seas is a very different experience from sailing on flat water in strong winds on a lake.

Anyone who masters the art of real surf-sailing will get tremendous satisfaction from it and will know what 'Boardsailing' really means. The ideal 'sea' is one which has regular waves, all moving in the same direction and a constant wind of about Force 4 or 5 at a slight angle to the waves. This will enable the board-sailor to surf down the front of the wave, preferably obliquely to it, in order to gain more speed. When the board accelerates quickly on a wave the sail must be heaved in immediately because of the change of direction of the *Apparent Wind*. 'Feeling' the waves and wind together is essential if you are to get the maximum performance out of the board, and a constant changing of body, foot and hand positions will be necessary. Perhaps the worst situation for a board-sailor is to find himself with big waves but little wind. It is a lot easier when you have some wind to 'lean on' to help you to balance.

Sailing in strong surf and sea can be very hard on equipment. Breakages are more frequent than under normal conditions and it is a good idea to take along some spare line or even a spare sail and daggerboard if conditions get really rough.

CHARCHULLAS

The most common damage (apart from torn sails) is to the dagger-board, and I would recommend what is known as a 'Charchulla' type

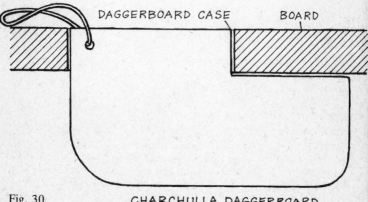

DAGGERBOARD CASE   BOARD

Fig. 30   CHARCHULLA DAGGERBOARD

(named after its inventor), a simple L-shaped affair, much safer in shallow water or in surf, where you can be swept in to the beach on a wave and hit the sand. (See Fig. 30.) The 'Charchulla' will not be pushed backwards, and therefore will not damage the rear of the daggerboard case, the part which most commonly needs repair. Some boards have, as you have seen, folding daggerboards, which should fold backwards when you hit the beach or an underwater object, but even with this type you must be very careful.

The sail, when thrown into the surf, will take a pounding and all ropes should be made extra secure or doubled up. Take care also to keep sand out of the sail-batten pockets by leaving the rig in the surf for as short a time as possible when near the beach. Sand and salt are the two worst enemies of the sail and you should try to wash the sail in fresh water frequently, particularly after sailing in surf. Let it dry thoroughly before folding it, and keep it in a dry place.

BREAKERS

One of the most difficult things about sailing in surf is getting out past the breakers. Both launching from the beach and sailing out against the waves can cause problems. It is best to assemble the board on the beach, making sure that the mast-foot is firmly in place, and the daggerboard half-way down; then tip the board onto its side or even upside down and, holding the 'uphaul' line, preferably with the sail just clear of the water, walk backwards into the sea until you are about waist-deep, then flip the board over at the opportune moment and jump on as quickly as possible. Knowing the right moment to start sailing will come with practice. You wait for a moment when the waves are smaller than usual and gather as much speed as you can **before** encountering the first wave. Always try to sail out through the breakers at right angles and always try to keep the sail full of wind. The board must be kept moving at all times.

Some top surf-sailors do not even bother with the daggerboard, unless they are racing and have to beat to windward. They manage to sail on a reach, as well as downwind without it, although this requires exceptionally good balance and co-ordination and is not to be recommended to those with little experience.

SURF

The 'Windsurfer' was, as the name implies, developed from the surfboard and is therefore at home in the surf. However, unless the sailor has had some experience of real surfing it would be advisable to study the sea's behaviour and wave patterns, and it is essential to be a strong swimmer before boldly venturing forth into the waves. **Boardsailing in surf should be tackled only when you are confident**

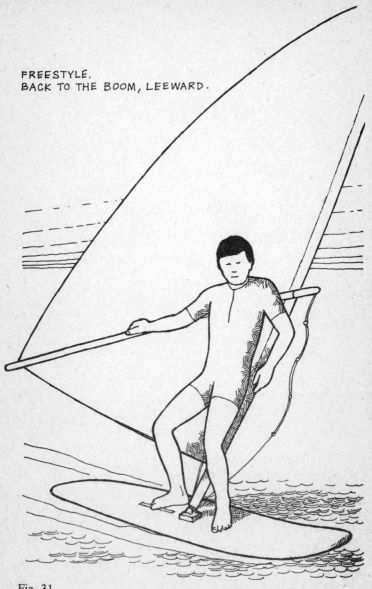

FREESTYLE.
BACK TO THE BOOM, LEEWARD.

Fig. 31

that you can handle the board well in strong winds and know exactly what to do in case of emergency.

Specialists in this type of sailing, in Hawaii for example, sometimes bend the bow of the board upwards by putting weights on it when it is upside down to increase the curvature. This helps prevent the bow from burying itself in the waves.

The latest development, which started in Australia and Hawaii, is called 'wave-jumping', and entails jumping off the top of a big wave in a wind of Force 6 or 7 and becoming completely airborne, using the sail as a kite. To do this they have specially designed boards with foot straps, to keep the 'pilot' in contact with his apparatus.

The boards used for this new development are different in shape from the normal ones, being shorter, with a turned-up bow and having the mast set much further back. They have a wider stern and twin skegs (one each side) as well as straps for the feet, and are reinforced to deal with rough landings.

FREESTYLE AND TRICK SURFING

Once you have learned how to handle the board under most conditions you will, no doubt, want to experiment and you will soon discover that the number of tricks and variations is endless.

The board can be sailed in almost any position, including backwards, half submerged, or even on edge. (See Figs. 31 and 32.)

The 'Freestyle' sailor can put himself in the most incredible positions: back to the sail, inside the wishbone, kneeling, sitting or lying down, or standing on the edge with the board on one side. If you think conventional sailing is difficult, then you should try this!

Competitions are held for 'Freestyle', and the sailor does a series of tricks, which should flow into one another, in front of a panel of judges who award points for various standard tricks plus marks for originality, fluidity and style; the method is similar to that used in judging ice-skating freestyle competitions or acrobatic skiing.

Fig. 32

RIDING THE RAIL.
(STANDING ON THE
EDGE OF THE BOARD).
SAILING STERN FIRST.

Chapter 10

RACING

Not everyone wants to sail his or her board in regattas. Many people are content to sail just for pleasure in their free time, but you may feel that you will get more out of the sport if you sail in company, or better still, participate in regattas. Racing is one way of keeping up interest on lakes or gravel pits, where such excitements as waves or surf are simply not available.

Boardsailing races are held regularly in most areas of the British Isles and there are now Class Associations for the more popular makes of board. The U.K. Board Sailing Association promotes the sport generally, regardless of the make of board. Racing a board can be great fun; very frustrating, very exhausting but very satisfying.

Apart from being able to sail a board well, there are many other factors which come into racing, and tactics count almost as much as fitness. You also depend, more than in dinghy racing, on what the other guy does. If he loses his balance and falls in front of you, it could cause not only one person to fall (you), but half the fleet as well. We all have to start some time, though, and you will find that most board-sailors have a sense of humour (they need it!), and they will usually help you if they can. You will also find that your own standard of sailing improves by watching more experienced sailors at close range and trying to copy their example.

COURSES

The Olympic course laid out for a race consists of a triangle of three buoys; their position will vary depending on the direction and force of the wind on the day. The starting point is an imaginary line drawn between buoy number three and a boat at anchor, containing the Race Committee. After crossing the starting line the fleet tack towards buoy number one, which has been placed directly to windward at a distance decided by the committee. If there is a lot of wind the course will usually be shortened considerably. On rounding the first buoy, the fleet turns right on to a broad reach and then gybes around buoy number two to make for buoy number three near the starting line. From here they again tack to the windward buoy and then double back and run *before the wind* to the third buoy again, before making the final beat to windward to the finish — an imaginary line drawn between the committee boat (which has moved) and buoy number one. (See Fig. 33.)

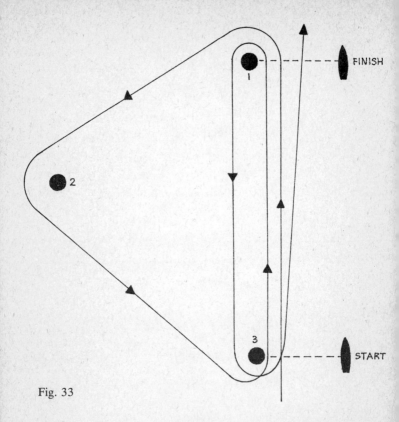

Fig. 33

RULES

The racing rules should be studied thoroughly so that you have no doubt as to who has the right of way, and what to do if you collide with a buoy, or hit someone's board etc.

There is usually a printed paper stating the starting procedure for each particular race, but if not, make sure you know the starting rules by asking someone in charge.

PRE-RACE CHECKS

Check all your equipment; see that all the knots are tied properly and that the ropes are secure and free from wear.

Clothing will obviously depend on the weather, but remember that once you are out near the starting line, sometimes a long way from the shore, it is too late to change, so it is better to take too many clothes than too few.

Give yourself time before the race, and sail out to the starting line in good time to assess the conditions (which might be different from those on the shore). Is the wind regular? Is there more wind further from the shore or less? Which direction are the waves coming from? Make sure also that your sail is tight enough, or slack enough, for the amount of wind. If the sail is too full, tighten the 'outhaul' and the 'downhaul' to make the sail flatter. This can be done fairly easily while on the water, sitting on the board.

It is best to sail up and down the starting line a few times to try to decide from which end you will start.

STARTS

A good start is very important. It is extremely difficult to catch up with someone who makes a perfect start if you are left behind on the starting line, unless he makes a mistake (and you don't)!

The first few attempts at racing can be quite hair-raising for the beginner. Suddenly, from out of nowhere, a whole pack of board-sailors are bearing down on you, claiming their 'right of way' in no uncertain manner, and you think you will be decapitated at least! There is almost always a favourite end to the starting line, the one which most sailors have decided offers the best possibility of a quick getaway, but it does not always happen that the leader crosses the line from that end. Sometimes there are so many boards crowded around the best end, all stealing one another's wind and juggling for position, that the chap on his own in 'clean' air is able to take advantage of the situation and sail clear of the pack.

You will normally reach and cross the starting line on the **starboard tack**, with right of way over the **port tack** (see Fig. 34). It's a good idea to wear your stop-watch on the right wrist, so that you can see it more easily while still looking forward. There is normally a five minute gun and then a one minute gun (although this is not always the case) and there is often some confusion and a lot of activity just before the start, with boards sailing in all directions, colliding and riding over each other. In the scramble for the starting line your sail is often blanketed by other sails and you are unable to manoeuvre because you depend entirely on the wind to do so.

TACTICS

The ideal start is one where you sail across the line at full speed a split second after the starting gun, with no one to windward who could blanket your sail. You sheet in hard and beat close to the wind,

Fig. 34

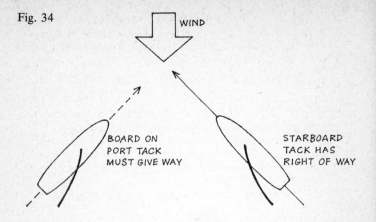

leaving the opposition in your wake. Sounds easy, doesn't it? Unfortunately it hardly ever happens that way, even to the experts. It requires a lot of practice, intuition and a slice of luck, as well as excellent sailing ability, to pull it off. Coming up to the windward mark, try to be on the starboard tack; otherwise you will have to give way to other boards with the wind already on the starboard side. The object is to round the buoy as close as possible and bear away immediately. This is easier said than done, of course. The board does not bear away as quickly as you want it to, and various techniques can be employed to get it to turn and sail on a reach, including briefly putting your weight forward and then crouching or kneeling down, dragging one foot in the water for a few seconds to force the board around.

When on a broad reach, lift or hinge the daggerboard up almost half way, and start to fly! It is not always advantageous to sail in a straight line towards the next buoy. You could first go wide, gybe before you reach it and then sail close to the buoy with the sail on the correct side for the next reach.

Once around the buoy number three (near the starting line) it is time to beat to windward again and this time you will know more about the state of the wind, if it hasn't changed since the first beat. See which way the leaders favour and follow them.

Theoretically, after rounding the windward buoy you should have the wind directly behind you and you would normally lift the daggerboard half way up or lift it out completely. If you are not convinced that you can do it successfully, then leave it right where it is, and practise some other time.

The competitors will be well spread out by this time and you should have plenty of time to manoeuvre, so just concentrate on sailing to the best of your ability and on keeping ahead of your nearest rivals as you sail the last leg to the finishing line.

THE FUTURE

You will have realised by now that racing a sailboard is not as easy as you thought it might be. You can never have too much practice, either sailing in races, alone, or just with friends.

It is physically a very demanding sport, particularly when you sail in a series of races one after the other, so the fitter you are the better. From sailing in local club regattas you could progress to National, European, or even World Championships, not to mention the Olympics. The sky's the limit, so good luck to you and welcome to our ranks!

VENTURE GUIDE titles include:

- Knots
- Small Boat Handling
- Wild Water Canoeing
- Chart and Compass
- Camping and Backpacking Cookbook
- Map and Compass
- Outdoor First Aid
- Survival and Rescue
- Weather Lore
- Jogging
- Backpacking
- Caving
- Hill Walking
- Lightweight Camping
- Orienteering
- Rock Climbing
- Winter Camping
- Walking
- Youth Hostelling
- Basic Skiing
- Cross Country Skiing
- Parallel Skiing
- Cycle Touring
- Sailing
- Snorkelling
- Cycling
- Trout Fishing
- Birdwatching
- Food from the Countryside